Copyright Notice

Copyright © 2012 by Charlie Valentino. All Rights Reserved.

Reproduction or translation of any part of this work beyond that permitted by section 107 or 108 of the 1976 United States Copyright Act without permission of the copyright owner is unlawful. Requests for permission or further information should be addressed to the author.

Charlie Valentino
UK
www.howtopickupwomen.org

This publication is designed to provide accurate and authoritative information in regard to the subject matter covered. It is sold the understanding that the publisher is not engaged in rendering legal, accounting, or other professional services. If legal advice or other expert assistance is required, the services of a competent professional person should be sought.

First Printing, 2012
ISBN-13: 978-1481913324
ISBN-10: 1481913328

Printed in the United States of America

TABLE OF CONTENTS

Introduction	5
What To Do At The Beginning Of The Date	6
What If Your Date Arrives Late	9
The First Conversation	11
How To Compliment Her	14
Establishing A Connection	19
Rapport Breaking	31
Qualification	35
Kino Escalation	46
Being A Leader	50
Investment	53
Body Language	59
Being Expressive And Projecting Yourself	65
Being A Challenge	70
What If She Says Something You Don't Like	72
What If She Asks If You Have A Girlfriend	73

How To Arrange A Second Date	77
Social Proof / Manufactured Demand	79
More On Being Busy	81
The Best Place For A First Date	83
What To Do When All Goes Wrong	85
About Your Looks	88
Questions and Answers	90
Conclusion	94
Also by Charlie Valentino	95

INTRODUCTION

I would like to thank you for picking up your copy of my dating psychology guide book for men.

There are two things I would like to have achieved by the end of this book for me to have done my job correctly.

Firstly, I would like any guy who reads this to have complete confidence on dates and with women in general. The things you're about to read will certainly enable you to be probably the single best date any girl you date will have ever had. There is great power in what you're about to learn so please use it responsibly. I'm sure you will.

The second thing I would like to achieve is for the ladies. We all just want happiness in this life, both guys and girls and a major part of this happiness is finding the right partner. If I can help a few guys to be great on first dates, an obstacle many can't get past then I'll be helping the ladies to find their dream guy in the long run.

I hope I can play a small part in this.

So let's begin our journey to becoming first date masters!

WHAT TO DO AT THE BEGINNING OF THE DATE?

Should you be arriving early, late or on time?

Unfortunately I've seen lots of bad advice about turning up late on dates, to show how much in demand you are etc. All that this will sub-communicate to the girl is how inconsiderate you are and that you're unable to manage your time properly. What else are you unable to manage properly if you can't be in a certain place at a certain time?

I always like to turn up a few minutes early if I know the place well and even earlier if I don't! That way I can go to the bathroom, check myself in the mirror and hype myself up. I'm not sweating anything and I can get myself excited at this stage. Then when the clock ticks over for zero hour I can naturally stroll into the venue on time.

If I'm not too familiar with the venue, for example if we're going to a museum (a great place to go for a first date btw) then I'll arrive around 20 minutes early, scope out the place simply for logistical reasons.

You don't want to be left with egg on your face for not knowing you had to pay for entrance (a common mistake in the UK as most museums are free entry) or for getting the opening times wrong. I like to ask the person at the cash desk about entry and opening times, I generally like to strike up a friendly conversation with the clerk at the cash desk and you'll see why below.

This little tactic is great at the cinema too. You can have a friendly conversation with any hot girl who works at the cash desk or who collects tickets. This has the added benefit that when you turn up with your date you can refer to your earlier conversation in some way that makes it look like you're old friends.

This is great for "social proof" and I'll give an example. You could ask the ticket girl before your date arrives what are the best films that are out at the moment. Later on when she takes your tickets and you're with your date you can simply say you decided to take her advice and that you'll be blaming her if the film turns out to be awful. Say this in a jokey way of course.

Your date will be left wondering just how you know her! This is great if she's a hot girl as it's social proof (more on this later) for you. Imagine if you went for a coffee or a drink at a bar afterwards and the exact same thing happened and you mention that you agree with the coffee girl, this is probably the second best Starbucks in town. Your date is going to think you're the friendliest guy in town and all the girls know you.

This is why you should always turn up early on a date and do your groundwork!!!

I also like to have a back up or contingency plan. You never know if your museum will be closed, she's already been to the museum or seen the film etc. Having something prepared in your head so you can suggest it and seem spontaneous is a great way of avoiding potential embarrassment. Remember guys, it's down to us to lead (more on this later) and not for the girl to do the leading for us! The easiest way to lead is to have a plan in your mind the entire time and of course also a backup plan.

However, when it comes to actually meeting up with your date, I always make sure I'm around 2 minutes early at the rendezvous and no more. This way you haven't been waiting around for ages.

WHAT IF YOUR DATE ARRIVES LATE?

Simple really!

I never really make a great big fuss over it! But you really shouldn't go overboard and make too much of a big deal out of it.

If you fail to mention anything however then she's going to assume you're a push over and that's not what you want.

The best course of action is to make a joke out of it!

When she finally arrives you can give her some kind of a nickname that pokes gentle fun at her lateness; Tania Tardy, Louise Lateness, Sarah Slow etc. You can then have considerable fun for the next few minutes calling her these names in good humour.

I like to also say in as nice a way as possible that her time must be more important than my time! This makes her feel a little bad, but you really must say it in a nice way. She should apologise and you can move on - other than calling her the nickname of course. Doing this will sub-communicate to her that you're a man who stands up for himself and that your time is valuable. These are of course qualities that women love in guys.

If she sends you a message saying that she's going to be really late then it does neither of you any favours to hang around for the next hour waiting for her to finally arrive at the rendezvous. By waiting around all this time, no matter how hot she is, you're really not painting yourself in a good picture and demonstrating that your time is valuable. She is also showing complete contempt for your time as well as being inconsiderate. If this happens to be the case on your date then it's best to let her know that you haven't got the time to wait around for her. The best course of action to take is to text her with something like, "I haven't the time to wait around, perhaps we should reschedule for when we both have a window!" (note the exclamation and not a question mark) Then leave her to do the rescheduling and put in the legwork. Because you've demonstrated that you don't stand for that kind of crap she almost certainly will feel inclined to chase after you.

When it's all said and done, as a high value man, you need to be expecting the same level of treatment from those you date.

THE FIRST CONVERSATION

The first conversation is normally filled with awkward small talk and nervousness from both sides.

This is the point where many guys put their foot in it (girls too in fact) which is a shame because this can be your chance to show you're a busy guy and get the date off to a flying start.

Take a typical first conversation that a guy and a girl will have on a first date, it'll go something like this:

Girl: So have you been up to much today?

Guy: Naaah nothing much really…You?

I'm sure you can probably relate to this, I for sure can!

Now keep in mind this is probably the very first thing you say to each other after greeting each other. Things are often awkward and you're both nervous. But by cutting this conversation short you're not helping yourself out. In addition and even more importantly, you're making it look like you haven't actually been doing anything all day!

This is crucial for attraction!

Busy guys are attractive!

Read the above line again!

So don't make it look like you haven't been doing anything all day! Now let's look at this alternative:

Girl: So have you been up to much today?

Guy: Well yeah, when I got up I dealt with all my emails, I've a few friends in Australia who've just gotten back in touch. Then my best mate Dave came over, we went for a jog and then for a quick game of Squash down at the sports centre. After that I went for lunch with a few friends at this awesome new place that's just opened up. Then, before getting ready to come and meet you I just had enough time to write a few reports and do the dry cleaning.

You see the difference already? Now you're painting yourself as a busy and an attractive guy?

You don't have to lie to them! In fact I never recommend lying to girls as you'll always get found out in the end but you can easily frame your mundane day into something that sounds exhilarating!

You can emphasize this even more by using descriptive words that enable her to gather pictures in her mind while you're speaking to her! This is something I'll touch on later as it's an extra bonus that will make you stand out.

Now compare the already pretty good answer above to this answer below:

Girl: So have you been up to much today?

Guy: Well yeah, firstly I wrote some emails to my friends in Australia, they've just gotten back in touch with me. We forged a friendship while backpacking in the Australian bush. Later my best mate Dave came over, we went jogging! I can't start my day without feeling the earth beneath my feet and the wind in my face. Then we went for a quick Squash game...I just love taking my anger out hitting balls against the wall. There's no better way to feel alive!

You see the difference? Using descriptive words in stories will enable her to make pictures of YOU in her mind while you tell the story! That's very powerful!

So to conclude this section...No you haven't been doing nothing all day! In fact you've had a very busy day and your date is very lucky you've managed to fit her into your very busy schedule!

HOW TO COMPLIMENT HER

Ok so now we're getting into some super psychological areas of the human mind which we can exploit to our benefit! What you're about to find out is the most effective way of complimenting a girl.

What you're about to learn here works incredibly well on first dates! But more than that it works like a charm in pick up situations too, if you're into pick up at all, which you should be. If you're in a bar, night club or even approaching a girl on the street then this technique can change things around in your favour with incredibly awesome power.

To explain this properly I'm going to have to try and relate it to something you will hopefully have experienced in your own life!

When I was a kid, I wasn't anything special; I was always a follower and was easily manipulated by anyone! Below is one of the ways it was done, although I doubt in all honesty my former manipulators knew what they were doing at the time!

We used to play Soccer in the park nearly everyday. Nobody ever wanted to be the goal keeper as it's the most boring position to play in! But the sneaky bastards could always have me volunteering to be the keeper and they did it like this...

Friend: You're really good in nets aren't you! You're fearless…I've never seen anyone so willing to stand in front of a Football coming for your face at such high speed.

Me: Thanks!

Friend: Yeah you can dive really far as well, it's really hard to score when you're in nets!

Now what my friends did was to complement me in an honest and sincere way! What's more is that they went into a little bit of detail as to WHY I was so good as a goalkeeper. For me this meant that I didn't want to disappoint them by altering this image they had of my goalkeeping skills.

Heck, I would even go as far as practicing my dives in my spare time so I could dive even further so I wouldn't alter that image they had of me as a fearless goalkeeper who could dive far! One time I even paid money to go on a goalkeeping course. That is how powerful a well-placed compliment can be.

Did your older Brother ever once say to you "I love you, you're so generous with your pocket money!"

This is the exact technique that older brothers have been using to fleece younger brothers of their pocket money for centuries!

So how can you use this to your advantage in the dating arena?

Well timing is important! It has to sound sincere and genuine for it to work, so pulling this out the bag when you've only been talking 2 minutes isn't going to work very well! You can however bring it out of the bag after about 5 minutes ☺. You'll have to use your best judgement!

Girl: So I went shopping with Sarah and we bought these new gloves, I've never seen gloves like them I just had to have them.

Guy: You know what, I can see why Sarah likes you so much, you're just so friendly! I've only known you a few minutes but you immediately make people feel at ease! That's a very rare thing in people these days!

Now girls don't ever get compliments from guys like this, they usually compliment them on their looks so you'll stand out again by doing this!

But you've just given her a sincere compliment about how friendly she is! Now unless you give her a good reason not to be friendly to you she's going to try her very best to keep this image of what you have of her in your mind! She's not going to want to disappoint you by being unfriendly! If it's a compliment that she believes to be true, or would like to be true, then she'll make it true.

> On the flip side and I digress here, but these images that people have of other people is why it's near impossible for guys to get out of the "friend zone" with hot girls they've been friends with for ages!
>
> It's just something for you to be mindful of that when guys give sincere compliments to girls based on their LOOKS then these girls are going to try extra hard to make sure that this image is never altered. This means dressing up and using makeup especially for guys they're NOT even attracted to!
>
> How crazy is that!!!
>
> But even more importantly this means the girl will almost never sleep with the guy as it means he'll get to see her in the morning when she looks rough and not her best self!
>
> You can indeed compliment a girl on her looks of course, but you shouldn't do it until after you've seen her without her makeup on i.e. you've just slept with her!!!

Now can you see how this could also work in a pick up situation?

Girls are often very uneasy with pick ups and for good reason, they're just not practiced at being picked up during the day! By using this technique while picking girls up you're practically commanding her to be friendly to you! It never fails to amaze me watching a girl who's nervous and closed up suddenly become friendly, talkative and chatty simply because you've told her sincerely how friendly she is!

You need to have been talking to her for long enough so that you've come up with a reason just why she's friendly! The reason is very important because if you don't have a reason why she's friendly then there's no way it can be genuine. She'll see through it in an instant! The compliment really has to be rooted, ie you have a reason for the compliment which will make it genuine and therefore extremely powerful.

ESTABLISHING A CONNECTION

It is getting a connection with a girl that is the single most important thing you could ever have in order to make it to date 2! In fact if you get this right then you won't really need anything else in this guide! Everything else would just be a bonus!

Connection is the reason why ugly guys get to sleep with hot girls!

Connection is the reason why so many guys end up marrying their existing female friends! Friends they weren't initially even attracted to! You do after all fall in love with the person underneath and not the looks right?

Unfortunately for connection, it takes a long, long time in many cases to build!

But what if there was a way to build instant connection? What if there was a way to have a girl fall in love with you almost immediately, or very quickly?

Is this possible?

I'm sure you've heard girls say about their boyfriend or husband that there was this instant connection and they just hit if off right away!

Fortunately this can happen and lucky guys can indeed fluke it!

But what if there was a way to get an instant connection with any girl and almost straight away?

Fortunately for you you're reading this guide!

You can build a connection with a girl by communicating with her innermost thoughts, desires, beliefs, motivations and experiences!

Read that last paragraph again!

If she believes that you understand her on these levels, these innermost levels which lie beneath her skin and deep in her head then there's no way that she's not going to feel incredibly close to you!

In general; men are not very good at this kind of thing, but girls are! This is why girls can often hit it off with each other right from the start!

Have you ever found yourself in a situation where you're telling someone, a guy for example about yourself at a party and you suddenly find yourself telling him even more about yourself simply because he comes across as being interested in what you have to say?

This is very hard to explain unless you can relate to it yourself!

Now I'm going to give you a few example conversations starting with how not to build a connection and slowly improve the conversation up until the final one which should be building incredible connection with the girl:

Conversation 1

Guy: So what are your hobbies?

Girl: Well I really like to go horse riding in my spare time, I've been riding ever since I was a little girl and we had horses on the farm!

Guy: Oh I don't really know anything about horse riding, what else are you into?

Funny as that may sound, this is what 99% of guys actually do when meeting new people!

Conversation 2

Guy: So what are your hobbies?

Girl: Well I really like to go horse riding in my spare time, I've been riding ever since I was a little girl and we had horses on the farm!

Guy: Oh I had a friend who goes horse riding, yeah she loves it! You two would probably get on great!

This is a little bit better, at least the guy is trying to form a bond! But why would she care about his friend who goes horse riding? She's never met her and probably never will! Most guys do this and I'm sure you have in the past. The thing that is happening in this conversation is that the girl is talking about herself and the guy is trying to relate *her* experiences to *himself* and the best he is able to come up with is that he knows somebody who goes horse riding.

I'm sure you yourself have many, many times been in a conversation with somebody and you're telling them about something that happened over the weekend. Perhaps you went rock climbing for the first time and you really enjoyed it. Then this person simply starts talking about how *they* have been rocking climbing and how fun it is. Suddenly the conversation has gone from talking about *yourself*, to talking about *them*. You see how this can be irritating on a first date? Do you see how this could kill any chances of forming a bond and connection with the person you're talking to, especially when you're doing it nearly every time the person makes a statement about herself. In fact this happens so frequently to myself when I'm speaking with other people that these days I simply tell them that they need to learn how not to turn things around to be about *them*, especially when I was just talking about how it was *myself* who just went rock climbing over the weekend.

Seriously, this is something that all guys do all the time and it can often take a large amount of conditioning to change our habits.

Now let's look at a situation where the guy is at least relating the girls answer to *her*:

Conversation 3

Guy: So what are your hobbies?

Girl: Well I really like to go horse riding in my spare time, I've been riding ever since I was a little girl and we had horses on the farm!

Guy: Wow so you're a horse rider? That's impressive! I would never have thought that about you when I first saw you!

Girl: Why would you say that?

Guy: I'm very impressed, I just can't picture you as the kind of girl who'd be such the outdoorsy type! Wow! Now you have my attention!

Now this is so much better. There's even a bit of banter in there, he's being playful and they're having a good time. If you even did this you'd be so far ahead of nearly every single guy on the planet.

Can you see how the girl is talking and the guy is not trying to relate the girls answer to himself having gone horse riding, but is instead picturing *her* sat on a horse and riding through the fields with the wind in her hair.

But you could take it even further and relate what she's saying even more to her!

Conversation 4

Guy: So what are your hobbies?

Girl: Well I really like to go horse riding in my spare time, I've been riding ever since I was a little girl and we had horses on the farm!

Guy: Wow! So you're a horse rider? I'm impressed, now you've got my attention! I would never have pictured you as the outdoorsy type when I first saw you, but it just goes to show you can never tell! You must really care for horses, and I've heard they're such a high maintenance animal to have, you must be an incredibly caring person. You must love the feeling of riding a horse at high speed through the fields? Tell me how that feels!

Now I know nothing about horses! But I've taken something that she says she's passionate about and I've related it to *her*! You really don't need to know anything about horses to be able to do this! I've certainly not been half listening to what she's saying while my mind searches through its database for that time when I was younger when I tried horse riding so that I could come up with some anecdote about what happened to *me* that one time. I've kept the emphasis and the conversation directed at her and her experiences.

By doing this you really are showing the girl you're interested in her and she really will feel different by talking to you.

> When adults talk about things that happened in both their childhoods an instant connection is formed!
>
> A very common theme is children's television!
>
> How often do you talk about your favourite TV programs as a child and end up feeling a connection with that person even if you've never spoken to them before?
>
> If you could take the same principle but apply it to something more than TV then you have a secret weapon you can use to your advantage!
>
> Try and find out if you had shared hobbies as kids!
>
> Did she go to girl guides as you went to boy scouts? Did you attend any similar sports or athletics clubs? Did you know any of the same people when you were younger? If you went to the same school then you will

> have known the same teachers! Did you go on holiday to the same place as children?
>
> Knowing this information, you can use it to create an incredibly strong bond very easily!

Horse riding is her passion and I've made a connection with her about horse riding and shown I'm interested! She'll no doubt be willing to talk for a long time about horse riding and all the guy in conversation 4 needs to do is look like he's really interested and connect on any more points made.

Now let's take another example of connecting:

Guy: You look very exotic, where is it you're from?

Girl: I'm from two miles up the street!

Guy: Very funny! But your parents - they must be from somewhere far, far away?

Girl: Yes, my father is from France and my mother is Italian!

Guy: Oh that's pretty cool! I've never been to Europe myself but I'm a big fan of Italian culture! They have a history that's just so remarkable and the Italian people are so proud of being Italian. It really shows in them I think! And you're half French too? That must mean you're really good at cooking then! I bet you're also a really fiery person who mustn't be messed with! I bet you've been to France lots of times?

Now most of the above is just me rambling on!

But the important thing is that I'm making a connection.

She's going to like the idea of being a "fiery person" and there's just no way she's going to disagree with being "proud!"

I would expect the girl to spend a good considerable time talking about France or Italy! And you should let her! Don't interrupt! She feels she can trust you because you've got this instant connection!

Ok, so let's take another example around something that's very important to all of us. We'll start with what most guys tend to do and we'll progress to what you *should* do.

Conversation 1

Guy: So what is it you do?

Girl: I'm at university studying to become a nurse!

Guy: Oh I've a friend who's a nurse. She lives in...

Once again, the average guy in this conversation is immediately relating HER career to HIMSELF! This really is the default position that most guys do instinctively which causes girls to wonder why they bother telling him anything at all.

Let's try again.

Conversation 2

Guy: So what is it you do?

Girl: I'm at university studying to become a nurse!

Guy: OK that's cool! That must mean you're a genuinely kind and caring person! You must just love helping people.

Girl: Yeah, I suppose I do! Yeah you're right about that!

Guy: So, tell me, I'm interested...What is it about being a nurse that you like so much?

When you take something like career, hobbies or interests and then you ask them what it is they like about that thing, you're really getting deep down into the girls mind. This is how you form close bonds with people.

Girl: Hmm I've never been asked that before. Well I suppose I like helping people, I get home and I know I've made a difference in a few people's lives. That makes me feel good.

Guy: Looks like I was right! You really are a kind and caring person aren't you!

I can completely understand that being able to form a connection with a girl, like I've just shown you will mean that you're going to have to, to some extent break your programming. It really is not natural for us guys to be told something by somebody and then to relate that piece of information to *them* instead of to *us*. It is after all easier to speak of ourselves than to see things from their perspective while they're talking. I know how it feels to have somebody talk to us about their hobbies; skiing, skating, football, Call of Duty, cooking etc and all the while our minds are racing around and are immediately picturing ourselves doing that activity. Our minds are databases that store information and memories and if we have a memory of having taken part in an activity that the girl is mentioning then that activity comes immediately to the forefront of our minds and then we just blurt it out without thinking. Because for whatever reason we feel we can connect with the girl if it turned out that we have also been skiing, skating or whatever it was she just mentioned. Often you can even see it on guy's faces when you're talking to them that they are thinking that they have also experienced that activity and they are just waiting for a break in your speech so they can add their experience into the mix. It's like a light bulb flicks on in their minds. To keep hold of that thought and to hold your tongue often means your mind goes into a kind of spasm, like you've been interrupted and you can't take your mind off that thought until you can reconnect the two ends. It's the same kind of feeling of being half-way through an important task and then suddenly having the phone ring on you. You'd be talking to somebody on the phone but your mind is still on the task you had to put on the back-burner and this causes to some degree consternation, confusion and distraction. Ever heard the saying that we guys can't multi-task?

You need to break this programming and stop thinking about yourself while the girl is speaking. Just let it go! Instead keep everything focused on her and she will never forget it.

What I would do now is reread this section again. Run through it in your own mind and get it down to an art! If you can master communicating with women on this level, then your first date will feel to her like you've known each other for a very long time.

You're now becoming an unstoppable machine in the dating world! From now on everything else you're going to read in this guide is an added bonus!

RAPPORT BREAKING

Now I'm going to assume you've done the above very well and the girl is thinking she's finally found someone who really understands her!

So how would she feel if she suddenly thought she could possibly lose you? This would be devastating!

If done correctly, breaking rapport or breaking the connection you've just made with her will make her be the one to chase YOU.

You see, breaking rapport forces her to try just that little bit harder to get you! She'll be wanting in a bad way to make things right again, because you just severed (or better put - lightly broken) your connection!

Have you ever been in a conversation with somebody you really like, maybe a hot girl and all of a sudden you've said something she didn't like? You can see she didn't like it by the look on her face or by her reply to you.

As a consequence you've found yourself having to make up for lost ground, you're apologising for what you've said and are in some way trying to make things better.

In other words she has you!

What if you can use rapport breaking on her to make her try real hard to make you happy again?

Read on!

The best way you can do this is by asking her qualifying questions! Don't worry I'll talk about qualifying in the next section (qualifying is possibly even more powerful than getting a connection!).

What you need to do is ask her a question where the reply could potentially make you think less of her! What is it that you're looking for in a girl? Think about it for a second!

If you hate smokers then you could ask her "do you smoke?"

She could then answer no, in which case everything is fine, move on! You could even make a little smile to show that her answer pleases you!

Suppose she answers "yes!"

Oh dear, this is not good!

What I would do here is show your displeasure in your facial expression. What I like to do is break eye contact for about ten seconds while repositioning myself on my chair. Basically I'm letting her see that what she's said has displeased me! I'm breaking rapport!

This is devastating to her if you've already forged a connection!

You don't even have to be horrid and say anything negative, you simply need to show a bit of displeasure by as little as breaking eye contact!

In fact it's my guess that her next words would be "but I'm really trying to quit, in fact I haven't smoked in 3 days!"

In which case you can show your pleasure again, she's made an effort to please you and you should repay her by smiling again.

Disclaimer: Never break rapport on something that is dear to her heart. It should only be done on superficial things. If you say you disapprove of her studying to become a nurse or of her horse riding then this will back fire on you in a big way!

I'll give another example of how you can break rapport using something very light hearted:

Guy: So what music are you into?

Girl: Oh I just love Celine Dion, I've been to see her twice and I have all her albums!

Guy: Haha are you joking me? Celine Dion? You can't be serious! She's terrible! Good god girl, I'm sorry I just can't look at you anymore!!!

Girl: Well I'm also into Cold Play, U2 and The Beatles!

Guy: Cold Play! It just gets worse! The Beatles however - now you're talking! I just love The Beatles!

You can see above that the girl tried to fix the situation by giving you more examples of music that she's interested in!

In turn you allowed her to fix the situation by agreeing with her that The Beatles are in fact the best band that have ever existed!

Breaking rapport is very effective on first dates and beyond because what you're essentially doing is positioning yourself ever so slightly above her. It's you that gets to decide if the date is going well! It's you that gets to decide if there's going to be a second date based on *your* preferences and not hers.

This leads very nicely into the next section which is all about qualification. When it comes to one secret weapon that can literally change everything, you can forget about everything else.

It's all about qualification!

Read on!

QUALIFICATION

Now I'm tempted to say that qualification is even more important than forging a connection with the girl, but for the simple reason that you won't get to qualification or really even need it if you build a good connection, I'm still putting the earlier section at the top of my list.

Once again, I will reiterate that building a connection is the most important thing to make a girl want to see you again.

But let's change the mindset for this section. For qualification is where YOU decide if you want to see HER again.

Qualification is something women are very, very good at!

They do it naturally! They do it all the time simply because they grow up with an expectation of what their dream guy should be like! Even if later on in their lives they become realistic as to what men actually are, when they are younger, girls still have this high expectation of what they want in a boyfriend or of men in general.

In fact it's tough luck for any guy who doesn't meet this high expectation.

In fact it's become a lot harder for us guys to "qualify" to their high expectations all thanks to Sex and the City and countless romantic comedies starring Jennifer Aniston, but I won't bore you by ranting on about that!

To put it simply, girls have in their heads a list of what we have to be like in order for them to be interested in us. It usually looks something like this:

1. Sense of humour

2. He MUST be a Doctor, Lawyer or run his own successful business

3. He must get me

4. He must be caring and sensitive

5. He must have an incredible body

6. He must be handsome

7. All my friends must also love him

This list will probably run on and on. The thing is that the hotter the girl, in most cases the longer the list.

In fact, girls will often go out of their way to find this information out about us and they'll be completely unapologetic about it too!

Take a typical conversation on the average first date:

Girl: So what is it you do?

Guy: I'm doing an apprenticeship with Auto Mechanics in town! / I work for the tax department / I'm an administrator!

Girl: Oh so how long have you been doing that?

Guy: About 2 years!

Girl: But you're also at Uni as well right? You are aiming for higher things yes?

Guy: Ermm well errmmm no.

In fact the guy above sensing the girls disappointment with what he does, seeing he could now lose her has to try hard to make up lost ground! But it's already too late!

Once he has to try to get her to like him again, it's already game over in most situations!

She has qualified him to her expectations and he did not match up to what she wants in a man!

The only way I can see him turning this around would be to show how proud he is of doing what he's doing. Showing how he's making a difference etc. Then bide his time and qualify her to HIS standards!

This is often hard for us guys! Remember her list above? Well this is a typical guys list:

    1. She must be hot!

Is it any wonder why girls have a big advantage over us? Is it any wonder why it so often appears like it's them that get to do all the picking and choosing instead of us guys!

Qualification is something that all women do! The hotter the woman the worse it gets!

But what if we could play them at their own game? What if we could qualify them to our ridiculously high standards of what we need in a woman for us to even consider them!

Well fortunately this is very easy once you understand the principles! We can play them at their own game and frustrate the hell out of them in the process!

You will find that if you're dating a not so hot girl, you won't need to apply much qualification. But trust me, as they get hotter, the more you'll need to qualify them!

If you're dating a girl who dates lots of guys, this is going to make you stand out so far and above any other guy she's ever met!

The first thing we need to do is make a list, just like how they have! You don't have to actually write it down, but just know what it is you want in a girl.

I mean it! What do you actually want in a girl?

This only really works if it's something not related in the slightest to her looks! Make sure that you're the only guy she's ever met who couldn't give a damn about her looks! The looks are just a bonus! What you really want, what you really need in a girl is what you have on your list!!!

1. She must be ambitious!

2. She mustn't smoke!

3. She must not be the one who simply follows all her mates, but does her own thing.

4. She can hold a conversation.

5. She's clever.

6. She likes to travel and discover new places.

7. She can't be materialistic, I need a girl who can be happy without all those flashy things.

8. She has to be spontaneous! I need someone who can run out in the rain with me when it thunders and just go crazy!

You see what a list like this does?

It doesn't matter how attractive she is! If she doesn't tick your boxes on this list then she doesn't get a look in! You'll be the only guy she's ever known who would turn her down simply because she's not spontaneous!

Hot girls are used to having all the power!

Now you've just taken that power away from her!

And because of this, she has no choice but to chase YOU!!!

And she WILL chase you!!!

She'll chase you because you're different, you're the only guy she's ever met that isn't drooling over her!

You're the only guy she's ever met who's used qualification!!!

So...now you have your list! How best to use this list?

Well the best way to use this magical list is to be blunt and just ask her!

Remember that the contents of this list are very important to you. So why not just ask her? She asked you about your job right? So play her at her own game!

Guy: You know, you're quite funny which I really like and you can hold a conversation! But what I really want to know is if you're the kind of girl who just loves discovering new places?

You need to make it look like it's important to you!

Disclaimer: You need to have built up a certain amount of rapport and have made at least some connection before using this! Otherwise she's not going to care whether she conforms to your standards or not!

No girl in the world is going to say "no" she doesn't like discovering new places! The fact is it doesn't matter! You're qualifying her based on something other than her looks and so far she's passing your tests!

After this initial little bit of qualification I would wait a while before trying it again. You could in the meantime find out what places she's discovered recently! And I'm not talking about the new nail painting place down the road!

By getting her to "explain herself" to you, by trying to impress you by telling you of the places she's discovered, you're forcing her to make a big effort to impress you.

Wait a few minutes and then throw in the big one, the money shot, the deal breaker!

Girl: So that's where I always go to get my nails done these days!

Guy: That's fine! Are you spontaneous??? I really like spontaneous people!!!

Again, no girl in the world is going to say she's not spontaneous. Even most guys like to think of themselves as being spontaneous, it is after all another word for exciting is it not?

Let's go back to the conversation where we left off!

Girl: Oh well erm, yes I suppose I am spontaneous!!!

Guy: Awesome! Tell me one really spontaneous thing you've done in the last six months?

Now just sit back and wait for her reply!

Remember to make it look like it's important to you that she's spontaneous. It has to seem to her like it's possible that the answer she gives might disappoint you. And that is an extremely important part of it!

If she gives a typical girly answer which is not something that excites you then you need to act genuinely disappointed (breaking rapport)!

Girl: Well I was bored last week so I just phoned my friend up and we drove 50 miles to the next town for a shopping trip!

Guy: That's rubbish! Give me something else! Something really cool that's going to impress me!

Girl: OK well a few weeks ago I was walking by a sign that said "join up for fencing lessons" and I thought, that's so cool, I've just got to give it a go, so I did!

The important thing is that if it sounds genuinely impressive, then you need to be impressed and you need to let her know how cool it is that she did what she did and that she has your approval!

Equally important is that if it's a load of crap and you're not impressed one bit then you have to tell her that that's nothing (in a half jokey, yet half serious way) and she's going to have to try harder to come up with something a little better!

Seriously! What you're doing is getting HER to impress YOU!

Think about all the times there's been girls you've liked in the past. You've gone out of your way to impress them by boasting about your exploits and everything else. What this tends to do in most cases is turn the girl off!

By the very fact that you're trying so hard to impress the girl, shows that she has you in her control, she has very little she needs to do to get you.

By phrasing your questions correctly and by being a little manipulative, you're actually turning the tables and getting her to impress you. Don't be turned off though like she would. You've been very clever and so you should reap the rewards.

When we try hard to impress somebody, it's because we really like them! We try to impress people because we want them to like us too. Qualification is how you get them to try and impress YOU, because on a deep down level you've positioned yourself slightly above them and they need to demonstrate that they are on your level.

By using qualification on a girl you're pretty much, for lack of a better expression, forcing her to impress you. If she's trying to impress you, then she must clearly like you!

This is how the rich ugly guy gets the gorgeous girl. Because rich guys naturally use qualification all the time. They've already been there and done that, they've got the car to prove it. If a girl is even to get a look in, then they're going to have to prove they're worth the effort.

One thing about girls, especially really hot girls is that they're very competitive! They have huge egos and this is how you use it to your advantage!

KINO ESCALATION

Kino escalation is something you should definitely be aiming to do! It is actually quite a broad area with literally hundreds of way of "doing kino" on a girl.

Imagine a date where you really like the girl but have been too nervous about touching her throughout the date.

When it comes to the end of the date, you're going to be even more nervous about making a move since no physical contact has been established in the run up. This is going to create a very intense moment at the end that could very likely end in disaster. Going for a kiss would be even more difficult to achieve.

The idea of kino escalation is that you establish right from the start small and tiny touches with her that gradually build up in a natural way so that everything appears smooth and normal. So going for a kiss at any time during the date should feel like a logical natural progression and therefore quite easy to pull off.

I highly suggest you begin kino escalation right from the very start of your date! Set the bar and continue! If done correctly then at no time should this be perceived as creepy, in fact she's more than likely going to be initiating much kino on her own.

When you meet and greet your date; shaking her hand and saying hi is fairly established! This is the first bit of kino which shouldn't be a problem!

However I suggest you take the first bit of kino a little bit further!

Instead of simply shaking her hand, you should also kiss her slowly on both cheeks whilst maintaining the hand shake.

After this, what I like to do, since I've already scoped the area out and I have the date planned is that I tell her where we're going. I will guide her gently with my hand behind the small of her back to lightly press her in the direction we're heading. I'll also leave it there for a few steps!

Tip: This will work even better if you're speaking about where you're going while you're touching her! It just makes the whole thing seem more natural and normal as well as providing a distraction while your hand is on her back.

Lots of my learned friends will even go one step further at this point and, as you'll be leading the way, you'll be walking maybe a pace or two in front of her. While you're in front of her you can hold your hand back as if you're with an old girlfriend and you're expecting her to take hold of it! You can leave your hand there as if expecting her to take hold of it.

Disclaimer: This is slightly more advanced! Don't run before you can walk. Unless you already know the girl well enough or have been having extending Facebook or text conversations.

For the rest of the date, you need to firmly establish yourself as a touchy feely kind of a guy, but in a smooth and natural way. You need to take nearly every opportunity to be making light, gentle and playful touches.

You can't be afraid here! You need to have total confidence and belief! If you feel weird about it then she will too! But if you start slow and build up, it won't feel weird.

If I know the area well then I'll point things out to her, maybe tell a little story about something that happened there. You can lightly turn her body around while you point. The elbow or lower back is always a great place to touch her when doing this.

Always open doors for girls! Not because of any social conditioning or politeness though. Do it so you can lightly push her through the door via her lower back.

If you get everything right that I've mentioned so far, particularly the part on getting a connection then trust me, it'll be her making the moves on you! All you have to do is start the trend and she's very likely to follow you and in fact lead the way with the kino herself.

And another thing; the first kiss should simply be a logical step on the kino scale. You can very well, and should go for this on the first date. It should feel natural. If it doesn't then don't worry about it. Do it when it feels natural, and this point certainly shouldn't be a tense moment right at the very end of the date.

I will say this again as it's a great little tip. It always helps if you're talking while you touch her because it shows that it's all natural to you and that you're barely even giving it any thought. It will make you seem more in control of the whole interaction and that you haven't really contrived the whole touchy feely thing. Most importantly of all, if you're speaking whilst you're guiding her around by the small of her back, or by touching her elbow or shoulder to emphasise a point, you're showing that you're not "getting off" on it.

BEING A LEADER

Leadership is one of the most important qualities any guy can have in life! When you think about those alpha males that women all love, one of the major qualities of any alpha male is being able to lead the group. In addition to having more success with the ladies, leaders also experience greater success in their careers. This is because leadership ability is highly prized and sought after in the workplace. There are few people out there who are able to organise groups of people and get the best performances out of them. Those few people who can do this go to the top. It should come as no real surprise then that on the dating scene, leadership is also highly desired in a man.

In fact leadership is one of the most attractive qualities a guy can have in a girl's eyes. When you are out on a date with a girl, you simply must be a leader.

Being a leader on a date should actually be quite easy! A girl's natural default position is to be submissive to the guy and to let him take control and lead the way. If leading isn't something that comes natural to you then you'd better learn to lead quickly.

Leading should begin even before the date has begun! It should be you who makes the suggestions as to what you should be doing on the date. Then as soon as your date arrives, you take control immediately!

Remember, you should have already scoped the area out and you should already know where you're taking her. Remember the gentle touches on her lower back to guide her. This is leadership and she will love you for it!

Being a leader on your date is much easier if you have a plan in your mind and so I recommend you go through everything in your head. This should also include a backup plan! If you thought I was being over the top at the beginning of this book by suggesting you go ahead and scope out and become familiar with your venue prior to your girl arriving then think again. If you think about it, being a leader is just another name for being an organiser. Which of course means you have to be organised! Have a think about any leaders that you know either in the work place or in your social circle. Are they also organised? If they are not organised then are they at least the person in your social circle who organises the group by telling everybody which bar you're meeting in, where you're eating dinner or which film you're going to see at the movies? I'm betting that he is.

However, you don't have to say things like "I'm hungry, let's go for a bite to eat at that Italian!" Although that is great leadership! Doing this only gives her the opportunity to say she doesn't like Italian food. It would be far better to give her the option. For example you could lead by saying "I'm hungry, do you fancy Italian or Tapas?" That way you're giving her a little say in it too whilst still doing the leading.

You can do the same thing on a date by deciding "spontaneously" (wink) to go to the cinema! "Let's go to the cinema! What do you fancy; the Johnny Depp film or the Matt Damon one?"

When you arrive at a bar or coffee shop, ask her what she wants to drink, then tell her to find your seats while you queue for the beverages. Be the leader! It should also be you who makes the suggestion as to when to leave the venue.

When you do leave you can decide spontaneously (wink) to take a walk in the park or along the river. Of course you probably had this planned out but making it seem spontaneous and seemingly making an on the spot leadership decision will count in your favour. Don't ask her, "would you like to go for a walk by the river?" Simply tell her, "Let's go for a walk along the river!" Trust me, she will be impressed!

Leading your girl on your date is actually very easy to do and don't forget, she will be expecting you to lead her. If you fail to lead her on the date then she's simply not going to feel the same amount of attraction towards you. Please get this easy thing right for the return on investment for the amount of effort it requires is great indeed.

INVESTMENT

Let me tell you about investment, because once you understand it, you'll finally understand just why it's so hard to let ex-girlfriends go. You'll then be able to use investment to your advantage to increase the chances of girls becoming more interested in you without them actually knowing why.

So what is investment? Put simply, it's everything up to this point in time you've put into a relationship. This includes; time, money and effort.

Investment, having put in your time, money and effort into a relationship is the reason why it's hard to let a girlfriend go as everything you've put into it up to that point will have been wasted, it will have all been for nothing. Investment, or lack thereof is also the reason why it's easy to let a girl go that you've only been texting a few times. If she doesn't text you back then it's no big deal since you've not put anything into the relationship thus far.

However, this becomes progressively a slightly larger deal to you the more you put into it. The more texts, the more time and the more energy of your mind simply thinking about a girl then the more painful it will be if she were to suddenly stop replying to your texts.

Keep in mind that you have to try and keep a balance of investment! If she realises that you're putting far more investment into the relationship than she is, especially in the early stages then you increase the chances of her not replying to your texts. This is because if you're investing more than she is then quite honestly, you're not being as much of a challenge as she would like.

Never invest more than she is especially in the early stages! This means your money! Share ticket prices, meal and coffee as well as cinema costs equally. You pay for the meal as long as she picks up the tab for the cinema is the best way of putting things!

Never let her realise you're putting more effort into the relationship than she is. If she asks you to drive 50 miles to pick her up because her car broke down then make sure she accompanies you to that new bar you've wanted to go to or otherwise does some other huge favour for you.

If you can get her to invest in you then you are effectively tricking her brain into thinking that she must like you. Get her thinking about you in her spare time, or while she's at work. Allow her to spend her money on you, buying you little gifts here and there. Don't always go to the bar to get your drinks, but make her do her fair share too. Make sure you order the drink in a particular way so she has to do a little extra work for you. For example, you only like your vodka and coke with ice and lemon! Allow her to cook for you whenever the opportunity arises for the same reasons.

Remember that the human being is programmed to value more what he or she has to work for! Get her to work just that little bit extra for you!

The most attractive women always have guys running around after them, offering to do anything for them just to get close to them. These are the guys who don't stand a chance with them because they are the ones who are investing too much into the "relationship" whereas the girl is putting absolutely nothing into it. It would be a very rare thing indeed for her to meet a guy who won't do her errands or buy all her drinks unless she does something for him first.

If you live several towns apart, then it would be a bad idea to go all the way to her town for your first date. Instead try and meet half way, or even better, slightly closer to where you live.

If she tells you she's going to a certain place to pick something up, then get her to pick up something very particular for you. This can't be something mundane like milk, but something she can only get for you because she just happens to be at this very particular place. For example, if she tells you she has to go to a certain town that has the best sweet or candy shop for miles, then tell her every time you're there, you always buy a certain thing as a present for your niece. She will be happy to help you out! But more to the point, she's probably going to have to go out of her way to get you that little gift!

If you're going to the cinema on your first date, then ask her if she can buy the tickets before you meet up because you have to first meet your friend. But of course, tell her the first drinks are on you!

Make her work for you and she will value you far more and she won't even know why.

The whole principle of investment holds true not just for the preliminary stages of your friendship, but also for while you're dating and even when you're in a full blown relationship. If your girl perceives that you are the one who is putting far more into the relationship than she is, then you're going to be thought of as "easy," which is not attractive for women. Women like challenges! If she is the one putting more into the relationship than you are then she will see you as just the challenge that she doesn't know she actually craves.

If your girl goes out of the way and does something nice for you, then don't be aloof as if you're used to this kind of thing. Let her see that she's made you happy. Investment should ideally be a two way thing, where you're both investing similar amounts in the relationship.

For now, the most important thing for you to realise is just how much you are putting in when compared to her. Don't go too far over that line where she'll see you as chasing after her. If you perceive that she has put that little bit more in than you have, then it's safe for you to advance towards that line of parity, or perhaps even a tiny bit beyond. But beware that once you cross that line, if you go a long way beyond then you are chasing her. This is not good. In this instance, simply sit back and allow her to put in a little more investment.

Investing in a relationship can be as big a thing as paying for dates, travelling long distances to meet her all the way to the little things such as initiating text sessions or calling her.

Just recognise (especially in the early stages) where you are and try and stay more or less level with her. Getting this wrong is a mistake many men make with women. They over invest in an attempt to "impress" her when in actual effect they're doing the opposite. In fact from the girl's point of view it may even come across as the guy trying to buy her affections if he invests too much. Take the example of my friend Chris who, no matter what I tell him, I just can't seem to get it into his head that if he wants to buy a girl's affections then he should at least wait until he's in a proper relationship with her and not a moment before. We never let him forget about the time he drove 40 miles to collect his date, drive another 70 miles to arrive at the races, where the girl then lost all her money, Chris (whose horse won) then gave her his winnings, drove to a third town, bought her an expensive meal, left the restaurant to find his car had been towed away for parking on double yellow lines and then paid for the girl to get a taxi home while he went to the impound lot to pay to have his vehicle back. Apparently she never returned his texts despite his utter kindness. What he did get though was a date bill of over £600 and a bunch of lads who will never let him forget. She on the other hand will no doubt have a funny story to tell the next guy she dates who will doubtless do a lot better simply by visiting the local museum followed by a walk in the park.

Now of course that is an extreme example and one which we never let him live down. But if he had made her go out of her way for him instead of the other way round then perhaps things would have been different.

BODY LANGUAGE

Of course, we all know that girls love confident guys! Confidence unfortunately is not something everybody is born with or attains to a high level during their lives either. If we come across as being unconfident, nervy or anxious during our dates, then I'm afraid, and I'm sorry to say, this can be lethal to our chances of success!

You can only really gain confidence, real confidence that is through competence. You gain competence obviously by becoming good at something. Remember how you were really nervous when you started to drive, but now you can do it, you're actually really confident at it. Well it's exactly the same with dating women. The more you do it, the more confident you will become.

For that reason, you should really consider getting as much practice as you can with dating girls, even if you're not that attracted to them. You'll be able to build up your social proof over time having dated many girls and of course you'll gain confidence! This way, when that girl who you really like comes along, you'll be much better prepared for the situation.

But did you notice me hint at something above? It's of course possible to fake confidence if you don't already have it in abundance, and faking it as actually quite simple in principal. Simply follow the traits below and incorporate them into yourself:

Leadership (see above)

Whilst not body language, it will make you the most confident person in the room, so I thought I'd include it anyway.

Take Up Space

This is just so simple! Next time you're in a bar, have a look at the guys and see who looks the most confident. It will always be those guys who're spreading themselves out. When you take a seat, widen your legs, prop one foot on the knee of your other leg. Lean back on your chair. Place your arm over the head of the chair next to you. This will make you look incredibly open and therefore confident. By opening yourself up like this, the incredible thing is, you will actually feel in yourself more confidence. Another thing you can do is to spread out your personal belongings around the table just that little bit more. This increases your personal area. Push your drink out further beyond what feels like your natural boundary. If your phone is on the table (and you don't live in a bad neighbourhood) then move it out a little further. Confident people take up space.

Widen Your Stance

This goes with the section above, but if you're standing and not sitting, then try standing with your legs a little further than shoulder width apart. This gives you a much more sturdy frame and makes you appear "rooted."

Eye Contact

This is a nice and easy one that hopefully you should already be doing. Your eye contact should not be intense, but instead soft and easy.

Control Your Movements

When you move, always ensure you're slow, calm and steady. When you move in fast and erratic ways, you're giving the game away as to how nervous you are. Slow movements of the head are especially important. Doing all this should really give you an air of confidence and control.

Hand Gestures

You can easily practice your hand gestures in the mirror. This really is simple to do yet easy to overdo so try and strike up a balance. Simply bend your arms at the elbow when you speak and make slow gestures with your hands. You can increase the movement and intensity when you make a point in order to emphasize it. Making nice, slow, comfortable and controlled movements with your hands is especially important because it will give you many opportunities to kino the girl. If you are naturally expressive with your hands and body when you speak then kino'ing her will be easy because you'll be presenting yourself with many opportunities to touch her during the course of a normal interaction. It really is so simple to make light touches with the back of your hand while you're making a point on something.

Don't Cross Your Arms

I used to teach a powerful technique to guys to help get women to open up to them and start being more friendly. I taught my clients that while they were on a date with a girl or if they were chatting to a girl in a bar and she had her arms folded then they could simply unfold them by complementing the girl on something and then giving her a high five. The girls arms almost never returned to the folded position and the girl would always open up and become friendlier. There have been many studies published that confirm this and more, that our body language actually commands how we feel in the moment and can therefore alter our state confidence. By folding your arms you are creating a wall between yourself and everybody else. This shows insecurity and discomfort. On top of that, it actually makes your whole attitude feel closed and shut off. Try speaking to your friends with your arms folded and then feel the difference when you unfold them, thus opening your body up. It's funny how things work sometimes.

Lower Your Drink

This will only apply if you're taking your date to a bar. The majority of people keep their drinks close to their chest at all times. Similar to having folded arms, this acts as a barrier between you and everybody else. We do this for protection because we are nervous or uncomfortable. Always lower your drink and keep it by your side. Confident people are open and don't need a wall between themselves and the people they are in the same room as.

Stop Fidgeting

This is a big one and something all of us do unconsciously. We fidget mainly because we're nervous. Nervousness just happens to be the exact opposite of confidence so I suggest you try and consciously cut nervous traits out of your being. Simply by incorporating the positive body language traits mentioned above into yourself, you'll feel more confident anyway and fidgeting should automatically be reduced on its own. However, if you have any nervous ticks or you tap your fingers or feet then you must try and stop doing this. Do you often play with your cell phone just to give your hands something to do? This is fidgeting! Do you often take small sips of your drink for similar reasons? Try and cut this out. Do you touch your face or cover your mouth when speaking. This shows nervousness in a big way and that you don't actually believe what it is you're actually saying. Liars cover their mouth when they speak without even realizing it.

Don't look down

This goes for when standing, sitting or walking. Looking down at the floor conveys weakness; defeated people look down. By holding your head up, you are exposing your neck, which evolutionary speaking is an extremely weak area. Therefore you are showing dominance by looking up because you don't expect any predator to dare make an attack on your weak and unprotected spot. Notice how Superman always looks up. He knows nobody is going to attack him and for good reason.

Learning the above body language traits and becoming comfortable with them is actually surprisingly easy. The return you will get from the small amount of time and effort you'll need to put in to get them down is perhaps the best return on investment you'll ever have in improving your life.

BEING EXPRESSIVE AND PROJECTING YOURSELF

This section leads on nicely from the section above! How you project yourself is another way you can make yourself appear more confident. The following traits are fairly simple to learn and you should try and incorporate them into your every day life. Doing so will make it appear more natural than simply pulling these tricks out of the bag for your dates:

Facial Animation

It is said that when we speak to people, the words we actually say account only for 10% of the overall message. While body language accounts for well over half, the exact number is debated. If you're curious what makes up the rest of the pie while we're speaking, it's a mixture of eye contact, smiling, voice tonality which we will cover in a bit and facial animation.

The next time you're speaking to the people around you, take note of their actual facial expressions. What do you notice? I'm guessing you'll notice that not many people's facial expressions actually change while they talk. Most of us tend to keep a normal and straight face while we're talking to people. What message does this put across? Well it says you're not very interested in the conversation for one, but it also shows a lack of confidence.

The next time you're watching TV, take note of newsmen and TV presenters and watch their facial expressions while they talk. These people are the masters of the facial expression. They have to be! They got the job because they're able to draw people in primarily with their faces.

Watch a movie tonight and watch the actors and how they use facial expressions to convey passion, interest, humour and a whole host of other emotions.

This is just one of the reasons why people on TV always come over as being super confident and interesting. These are no doubt traits that will be greatly advantageous to us on first dates.

You need to get into the habit of showing your emotion and interest in people when you speak to them by using expressive facial signals. In all honesty, not many people do this out in the real world and by being one of the few who do, you'll stand out for sure.

Practice talking in the mirror, don't laugh, I mean it, it'll be a great exercise for you. You need to get the balance right so that you don't look like you're overdoing it but instead it should come over as being completely natural.

This is so easy to do and it'll make such a huge difference to how you come over to the girl you're dating.

Voice Tonality

The speed and tonality in which we speak together make up the rest of how we are perceived by others while communicating. The speed you speak at and your tone of voice together are actually a lot more important to showing how confident and interesting you are than what it is you're actually saying.

Once again, I'm going to ask you to pay close attention to TV presenters and news anchors to learn from the masters.

Voice tonality in particular can be used to great effect. By alternating your pitch you will come over as being extremely interesting simply because practically nobody does it. You can use voice tonality to emphasise points and a lot more on top of that. The best way to describe how you should aim to sound is by saying you should talk with emotion. If you'd like to hear a great motivational speaker who can draw you in through voice tonality then watch a few Youtube videos featuring Tony Robbins.

With regards to speed, I'll say you should speak in a slow, calm and controlled way. By speaking slowly, you're showing your dominance and confidence. Have you ever spoken to somebody who speaks really quickly? This always makes them come over as being nervous and even erratic which clearly is not good.

In general you should always try and speak slowly and calmly however I'll also say that in order to sound a little more interesting, there's nothing wrong with alternating your speed a little bit just like you should be alternating your pitch. However, don't overdo this and use your best judgement. Think Brad Pitt in Fight Club!

I was advising one of my friends on voice speed. He is one of those who stops people in the street to sign them up to a charity. His problem was that people kept on walking away from him when he spoke, a big problem for many of these street charity people. When I saw him in the street working, I told him his problem was that he was speaking too quickly and he'd have more success if he slowed down a little. Because he spoke really quickly, he gave off the impression that what he had to say was not important and that speaking fast helped to get his message over before people had the chance to run away. He confirmed to me that this was why he spoke quickly. When I told him to slow the speed he was speaking at he told me he was afraid people would get bored of him and the end effect would still be the same. I made him realize that those thoughts were killing his confidence. Together we practiced his message in a more slow and controlled way. The results? Over the next week he had an increase of around 50% in signups.

Why was the increase so dramatic? Because by speaking slower, you are demonstrating complete confidence and belief in what you're saying.

As I mentioned earlier, if you adopt these confidence strategies into your being, you will actually feel real confidence within yourself. This will then further perpetuate more confidence from you. It's a positive spiral that all begins by learning all the above methods that help you appear confident on the outside, that will of course make you feel confidence on the inside. This is extremely important for when you're on your dates because we all know that women really love confidence in men. Get these tips down and you'll be so far beyond most guys out there.

BEING A CHALLENGE

There is some stupid philosophy out there that to keep girls interested in you, you have to be mean to them!...

"Treat them mean, keep them keen"

...is a saying we have here in England.

This is complete crap. Being horrible to girls is one way to keep low quality girls interested in you for sure! But by using the strategies in this guide you should be aiming for your dream girl because they are the ones you'll be able to get.

To keep girls interested in you then yes, you do have to be a challenge but no you do not have to be a complete idiot!

The best way to be a challenge is by being a genuinely busy guy!

Girls should ideally have to be competing for your time with all the other stuff you've got going on in your life!

Remember the section on your first conversation? Well this all ties in nicely to that!

Busy guys are attractive guys!

Let her realise that you've got so much other stuff going on in your life; hobbies, courses, work, friends, sports etc and possibly even other women (more on this in a bit) that she's going to have to battle to see you!

Of course you're probably going to want to see her again, so don't make things overly tricky!

Tip: Always carry a diary with you on your dates! So that when you arrange date number two (and you always should arrange it during date 1, again more on this soon) you can quite easily scroll through your diary and make it seem like you're busy!

WHAT IF SHE SAYS SOMETHING YOU DON'T LIKE?

Well first of all you should definitely be hoping for an opportunity to disagree with her on something! It provides a great opportunity to show you're not like all the other guys who agree with her on everything!

Most women just love a good argument!

Disagreeing with her on an issue will give her a chance to actually have a debate with you, to flirt with each other and to allow you to stand out in a positive way from all the other guys!

Just don't start an argument for the sake of it. Please make sure it's about something genuine!

For first dates however, I wouldn't recommend you having a heated discussion about anything too heavy and serious. Stay away from politics and religion to be safe unless that's something which is really important to you!

WHAT IF SHE ASKS IF YOU HAVE A GIRLFRIEND?

Well firstly if she asks you this then congratulations!

It's a sure sign that she's more than interested in you!

In fact this may well crop up even on your first date!

So don't panic when it does crop up! Be expecting it!

If you've made your list and you're looking for that perfect girl, then chances are that you're going to be seeing quite a few different girls! There's nothing wrong with this, in fact it's quite alright. You are after all looking for that one, special, perfect girl that's going to make you happy!

What most guys would do in this situation would either lie to her and say that they're not seeing any other women, or they would boast about how all women love them! Either way and you're going to lose out!

This moment will most likely arise on a first date after you've kissed! This is how the conversation should go:

Girl: So do you have a girlfriend?

Guy: I don't have a girlfriend no, but...I am dating! I'm trying to find that one person who's going to make me happy so yes I am seeing who's out there!

Do you think for one minute that being the one guy with the balls to be bluntly honest and truthful about seeing other girls is suddenly going to make her not want to see you again?

Not a chance!

There is a popular saying out there that goes something like this:

"Men have huge egos!"

Well I say that there's a less popular but even more truthful saying that goes like this:

"Women have even bigger egos!"

The fact you're seeing other girls will in fact, as long as you're honest and sensitive about the issue make her even more attracted to you!

Girls are incredibly competitive with each other! They all want to believe that they can be the one to get you! To tame you so to speak!

The funny thing is that once again, the more attractive the girl, the better this can work! Attractive girls are not used to having to compete for men with other girls. They always have men running after them!

You must however be sensitive and logical in how you put it over to the girl!

But what if you're not seeing any other girls? What if you've not had a date in years?

Well on the reverse side, letting girls know this and letting your date know that you're not popular with the ladies can have its consequences! Women like to think that their man is desirable! And the best proof of how desirable a man is is how many girlfriends he's had, or how pretty his last girlfriend was, or how many girls he's seeing right now!

There is more stupid advice out there about this! This is why men should not read girly magazines. I've read that men should not mention ex girlfriends on dates! This is bad advice!

Men should not boast about their conquests, true! But if the conversation comes up then they should not shy away from it! In fact you should use the situation to your complete advantage!

Women are the exact opposite to men! We men like to think that the girls we like have not had many other boyfriends, and if they have then they'd better be little wussy guys with nothing going for them! We'd be intimidated if he was Mr Universe who also owned his own company.

However women are the opposite! They like to think that all your ex's were pretty, clever and wonderful people! If they weren't all these things then what does it say about them?

If a girl asks you about your ex, which they often do even on first dates, then don't do what other guys do and shy away from the subject just because you've read bad advice! What you should do is make your ex out to be a wonderful person, with lots going for her. She was beautiful, funny and you got along great. But after a year of going out, you realised she wasn't the right person for you. You are however remaining friends!

See how much better that sounds and will make you appear over the alternatives!

You need to be making a concerted effort to be dating as many girls as possible! At least until you find that special girl you want to be with! Doing this will make you appear very attractive to women.

HOW TO ARRANGE A SECOND DATE

I used to hate all that crap about will she phone or won't she! I can guarantee you she hates it too!

It's so simple to just cut the crap and be done with this!

You'll be spending a good few hours with her on your first date so you'll be finding out what each other likes along the way!

This is plenty of time to find common ground!

Find out what it is you're both interested in and do something about arranging a second date based on that common interest!

If it's a common interest and you mention it as it's brought up, then this is an ideal time to mention doing that activity together in the future!

There's really no need to ask her at the end of the date if she'd like to see you again or even worse, wait for her to ring or text you for days afterwards.

Girl: I just love Matt Damon, I've got all his films!

Guy: Yeah I just loved him in the Borne series, I've seen them all like 4 times!

Girl: Yeah he's so cool!

Guy: Have you seen the new film he's in at the cinema yet?

Girl: No is it any good?

Guy: I don't know I haven't been to see it yet! You know what…we should defo go next week!

Or

Girl: Yeah I love all jazz music!

Guy: Yeah, have you ever been to Club Hifi, they play awesome jazz every Wednesday night"

Girl: No I've never been!

Guy: Well then we've got to go…this Wednesday!!!

Remember I told you to keep your diary with you! This is where you pull it out and flip through it all, making sure to let it seem like you're dead busy!

Arrange your dates ahead and you're sorted! It's so easy there's really no excuse!

SOCIAL PROOF / MANUFACTURED DEMAND

I don't know if you've ever heard of social proof?

Social proof is where you demonstrate to girls that you're popular with the women, thus perpetuating your attraction in a positive spiral!

You never do it by boasting about how many women you've slept with!

The right way to do it is through subtlety!

A guy who walks into a bar with 5 women has high social proof!

A guy sitting in the corner alone, staring at the women has low social proof!

So how do you demonstrate high social proof on a date when you're alone with a girl?

I briefly touched on this subject above! When you refer to your ex's in positive ways! Albeit only if she asks!

Well how I like to do it is by briefly and subtly referring to my female FRIENDS through stories! You don't need to have been in a relationship with them!

There's one word for a guy with no female friends - Creepy!

You can make girls feel more attracted and comfortable with you by mentioning your female friends in stories:

Girl: So what are you doing tomorrow?

Guy: Well I promised my friend Jayne we'd go shopping for a new laptop! You see, she knows nothing about computers, and I've had a laptop for years so I thought I'd help her get a great deal at the store.

Or...

Girl: So what are you doing tomorrow?

Guy: Well a bunch of us are going out to a few bars tonight, my friend Kelly said there's this new place in town called The Silo so me, Kelly, Dave, Jayne and Mary are all off to check it out!

Use social proof to your advantage! It can also be used to highlight your busy lifestyle!

MORE ON BEING BUSY

I've referred numerous times to being this great, busy guy who ticks all her boxes!

Well guess what? If you actually were this great busy guy then there'd be no need to fake anything whatsoever!

If you fake it then you'll only be found out in the end!

You only live once my friends so why not just do all those things you actually want to do!

Make a list! Yes I know another bloody list!

List all those things you want to achieve and set out to do them!

When I was 23 I took up breakdancing and I've been doing it ever since! When I was 26 I started writing screen plays, I've written 3 of them and I hope that one day they'll be made into films. When I was 29 I started to learn Italian, I'm now fluent, I intend on learning more about Italy, their culture and their cooking. I'm now 30! Right now I'm trying to help other guys find their dream girls by writing informative guides! When I'm 32 I intend on starting either fencing or hang gliding I haven't quite decided yet!

What I'm trying to say is that you have to be this person that girls want to be with! There's no need to fake anything if you live the lifestyle already! My girlfriend absolutely loves telling all her friends that she's going out with an Italian speaking breakdancer! How many other guys can say that about themselves?

It doesn't matter what in the hell it is that's on your list, but make a list and make it exciting for you! You'll be so far in front of everybody else who's hobbies only include watching TV and playing on the Playstation!

Besides all this, if you're out there doing all these exciting things, and attending classes then these are the places where you meet girls my friend! But what's better is that you'll be meeting them in friendly environments where you already have so much in common!

Just go for it!

THE BEST PLACE FOR A FIRST DATE

For me the best place to take a girl on a first date is the museum! Any museum will do!

You'll have lots to talk about, there'll be no awkward silences as you can just voice an opinion on a particular exhibit!

You'll be able to walk around freely and easily which will enable plenty of opportunities for kino escalation. You'll also be able to lead her around the place, something we've already covered so you know how important that is.

When you're finished at the museum and you're both comfortable with each other, then you should go for a walk along the river, in the local park or around the sites of the town. Then take her to a bar or coffee shop to get a little more intimate.

Having your first date in a museum will really make you stand out from all the other guys who simply go to a bar. However I understand that's it's not always practical if there are no decent museums around or if you both have busy work schedules.

If this is the case with you, then the second best place to go on your first date would indeed be a nice, chilled out and relaxed bar.

But if I were you, I would certainly find some interesting museums in your local area to take her to because they really do provide you with great opportunities to pull off the advice I've shown you in this book and to showcase yourself in your best light.

WHAT TO DO WHEN ALL GOES WRONG?

You will from time to time have those bloody awful dates! It's just one of those things! Not everybody is compatible after all so don't feel bad or beat yourself up over it!

You may get the impression the girl is not that interested in you, and a good indicator of this is if she suddenly stops giving you eye contact! Other times you may just get the general feeling that she's not interested! Your instinct is a valuable tool here!

This is all fine if you don't really like her much either as will often be the case!

But what if you do like her?

Well as I said, this is just one of those things you'll have to live with! If you do everything I've said above then you minimize the chances of this happening.

I have on one occasion been practically marched out of a girl's town by her due to a simple misunderstanding:

Girl: So what are you doing next week?

Me: Well to be honest with you, I'm normally just too busy!

The date ended about 30 seconds after this! I was simply answering her question whilst having a momentary lapse of concentration following an hour in a museum and a meal. It was only much later whilst driving home when I realised she probably liked me and was merely trying to set up a second date!

What I did was take the best course of action and was a man about the whole thing. I simply texted her telling her what I think happened and that I wasn't "blowing her off" but was simply answering her question and that if she wanted to hang out again then that'd be cool with me. I then left it!

I didn't hear from her for about 3 months and was then surprised to get a text!

Again the girl's ego at work! I'm pretty sure she couldn't understand why I wasn't texting her repeatedly given that she was a doctor and a very hot one at that!

One time, with a different girl, as soon as I mentioned I was still living with my parents, I noticed an immediate change in her attitude and a total loss of eye contact for the rest of the evening.

We didn't part until an hour afterwards! I spent that hour trying to turn her round with funny stories and by following lots of other bad advice I'd read in other books. I just wish I'd had the balls at the time to have stood up and said that I realised I must have said something to turn her off me, that we're both wasting our time and wish her a good night while we still had respect for each other!

When everything goes wrong, sometimes walking away whilst remaining polite about it is the best course of action and sometimes this drastic action can have a remarkable turnaround effect!

ABOUT YOUR LOOKS

It's true that looks are important to girls, but they become far less important when you apply what you've read here!

Your physical shape is much more important than your actual looks. Fortunately with a little work this can be changed and made into a complete positive for you. Join a gym and get some good advice from a personal trainer! Gyms are also cool places for meeting girls. Why not join a few aerobics or spinning classes and meet the women there. If you really want to get in peak physical condition as quickly as is humanly possible then I highly suggest you take up HIIT (High Intensity Interval Training) sprinting. It simply is the best weight loss method in existence hands down. I can recommend the book HIIT by James Driver on this very subject.

After your physical shape comes your fashion sense. With a little money and some good advice this can be a total asset for you. Of course your overall grooming is very important too. These are all things you have complete control over so there is little excuse for guys not getting the girl simply because of how they look. How you make use of what you have is much more important than your physical beauty.

If looks are still an issue for you then they will be an issue for her too! If something is holding you back then deal with it! Surgery is a last resort of course, but if you feel that getting work on your teeth or complexion will improve your confidence then this is some action you have my blessing on.

Questions and Answers

I have received many questions and lots of feedback from my readers. Here are some extremely common questions with regards to the first date which I shall now answer.

Question: Do you have any more examples of turning a date around when it goes badly?

This part I'm writing now is actually an update to this book since I've been back on the dating scene following a relationship. When I first started writing this book *First Date Tips For Men*, it was in 2009. Now in 2013 I have written a total of seven self-help books for men, as well as numerous fiction stories. I now call myself a full time author. One girl I was on a date with asked me what I did for a living and I told her. I then elaborated, telling her that the work of an author involves sitting in a quiet room trying to write. Well for this particular girl, it seems that this kind of existence wasn't a thrill for her and she told me, ten minutes into the date that she'd already made her mind up about me and that I wasn't going to be the guy for her.

I told her that I was glad she was honest about telling me that my work would put her off. I then went on to say that I don't make my mind up about people so quickly, I was still deciding about her right up until the moment when she said she had already made her mind up about me and that now *I* was put off. Within five minutes, I actually had her apologising to me and she spent the rest of the date chasing me.

I suppose the moral is that yes you can indeed turn things back around when things start going downhill, but you need to be willing to lose the girl in order to do that. This will often mean being a man and telling her that she has disappointed you.

Question: We've decided to go to a concert on our first date, but the tickets are quite expensive. Should I pay?

There is nothing wrong with paying for your concert tickets. Besides, it won't look too great if you demand half the money from her upfront. She will be well aware of the investment you've put into the date. Maybe you can have her drive you both to the concert so she is having to invest a little herself. You should also say to her, "I'll buy the tickets if you get the first drinks at the bar afterwards."

Question: There's a girl I really like and I'm not sure if she likes me. What should I do?

Well this is a little beyond the scope of this book. For this little problem I recommend my book The Alpha Male System which I wrote to get women chasing us guys and not the other way around. Ideally this girl you like would already know you're in the top 0.1% of guys out there in which case she should be chasing you. That is what that book is about.

Question: I'm just so nervous, I don't know what to do with myself! Charlie, help me!

I know how it feels. It's perfectly normal to be nervous before a first date and it seems to be worse the hotter the girl is right. This is why I suggest going on as many dates as you can so you become desensitised to the feeling of fear. This way you'll also be more in control when that rare girl you really like comes along and you'll be on top form.

For now though, the best advice I can give is to have a PLAN! Plan your date, including a contingency plan and meet your girl fully intending to lead her. Concentrate on making a connection with her as I've stated above. Everything I wrote there four years ago of course still holds true today, and it will continue to do so a hundred years from now.

Question: Charlie, we had a great first date but she's not replying to my texts. What can I do?

Read again the section on *investment*. Are you putting more in to the relationship than she is? The fact you're texting her and she's not replying in all probability means you are.

The best advice is to date more than one girl so you're not investing too heavily in any one person, until the point when she deserves it.

Conclusion

Thank you for reading this guide! We've covered some fairly big principles. I now suggest you read through it all over again. You should also check back before your next big date and go through again any areas you're not totally sure about, especially the chapter on establishing connection.

When you think about it, it all boils down to being the best person you can possibly be! Be the guy that girls actually want to be with! There's very little trickery involved!

With what you've learned in this guide you have everything you need to be the most memorable date your girl will ever have.

The most important step now is to take action!

I wish you the best of luck!

Charlie Valentino

Also By Charlie Valentino

Meet Women on Facebook

Meeting women on Facebook is easy, as long as you know what you're doing!

You need a profile that makes you stand out from the rest of the guys out there, who message random girls all the time hoping for a response.

Learn how to craft the best Facebook profile possible to enable picking up girls on Facebook easy!

After that, use our Facebook pick up lines to pique her interest and have her impatiently message you back.

It's all here in Meet Women on Facebook to make Facebook pick up easy for any guy out there.

No matter if she's an existing Facebook friend, a friend of a friend or you have no connection with her whatsoever, discover the complete formula from the first message to the first date now.

With most of the world's hot girls on Facebook, Facebook dating is the future! Don't miss the boat on this one!

Confidence for Men

This revolutionary book which aims to help men from all walks of life improve their self-confidence contains 24 chapters of easy to implement tips and strategies.

Discover the subtle body language traits which all confident men have and how you can use confident body language to actually fool your brain into thinking you're a confident man.

Learn about becoming a leader, one of the most important things all confident people have in common.

You'll also find out how to create the best possible social circle, the importance of identifying and cutting out negative people who bring you down and instead finding and including those people who'll add to your life.

Building self-confidence to last you the rest of your life begins with taking action! Confidence for Men emphasizes the importance of taking action. That action starts here!

Destroy Approach Anxiety – Effortlessly Approach Women without Fear

Approach anxiety is something the vast majority of aspiring pick up artists suffer from when starting out approaching girls. If we can't get over approach anxiety, our first major stumbling block in the world of pick up then we're not going to meet many attractive women.

Destroy Approach Anxiety covers this subject so you can get over this easily and then on to the good stuff which is approaching women without fear.

Find out the true reasons why we suffer from approach anxiety, it may surprise you. One of the author's beliefs is that it's the overloading of information in our heads in an attempt to gain perfection before we've even made our first approach. This is impossible!

The author emphasizes the importance of keeping pick up as simple as possible, especially when suffering from approach anxiety. He gives numerous strategies for maintaining the perfect pick up, without overloading the head with too much information, which you can't possibly act on when under pressure approaching hot women.

Destroy Approach Anxiety should be the first PUA book you read as it will help you find approaching girls in the street as simple as possible by getting you in the right frame of mind.

Direct Day Game Method – Pickup Girls on the Street, at the Mall or Coffee Shop!

Direct day game allows guys to cut the crap and just get to the point! It's just you and her in the moment! That's why it works so well, women respect guys who put themselves on the line! - Charlie Valentino.

There is nothing quite so empowering as being able to walk straight up to any girl in the middle of the street and tell her you think she's stunning! This is what

Charlie has been doing for years and he shows you how you can do it too.

Using the direct approach on a girl during the day in the street, coffee shop, mall or university campus is about as straightforward as pickup gets. For this reason Charlie Valentino says it's the best method for beginners and newbies or for those suffering from approach anxiety. Because the direct day game approach for meeting women really does cut the structure of pick up right down to its bare bones. There will be no rubbish flying through your head, no lines, stories, routines, tips or tricks. It's just you and a very attractive girl in the moment.

Charlie shows you how it's done with ease and a high probability of success!

Online Dating For Men

1 in 5 new relationships now begin from an online dating site. Given that only a few short years ago this figure was zero, this is quite impressive. It is estimated that within a few years, the vast majority of new relationships will begin through meeting on an online dating site!

Having said that, 95% of all men who sign up to an internet dating site will give up within one subscription term.

Charlie Valentino has now authored his sixth relationship book for men, aiming to help guys meet their dream girl whether on Match.com, Plenty of Fish or any other online dating site.

In this book you'll learn:
- The mind set and strategy you must take to set yourself apart from all the other guys online.
- The pitfalls of online dating and why most men fail.
- The webs best online dating sites and which ones to avoid.
- All you need to know to create the single best profile that will stop women in their tracks. Crafting that perfect profile is the single most important thing you must do to ensure women return your emails. Charlie Valentino previously authored Meet Women on Facebook and is an expert on creating enticing online profiles.
- Discover the many mistakes that men make with their profiles so you can ensure you don't make the same mistakes.
- Learn how to craft the perfect opening email to send to girls to give yourself the highest possible chance of receiving a reply.
- Charlie also shows you his tried and tested cut and paste email system.
- See evidence of what 99% of guys are doing and why it's impossible for them to stand out and make any impact. This is valuable information to know, so you don't do the same.

Online Dating For Men contains all you need to know in order to attract women online, improving dramatically your chances of dating as many women as you like through online dating websites.

The Alpha Male System

The Alpha Male System

8 Elements To Becoming Alpha Male!

Charlie Valentino

The Alpha Male System concentrates on eight fundamental alpha male elements which are visible as well as desirable in all leaders of men, which women also happen to crave in abundance.

In the days of the "metro sexual," men with alpha male traits and qualities are becoming rarer and increasingly more sought after.

Those few alpha males who can lead people, command respect and change the dynamic of a room simply by walking in it have all the luck. Or is it luck?

Discover the eight alpha male elements which will change your life along with detailed plans to attain them.

Becoming an alpha male is possible for most people, as long as you're willing to put a little work into yourself.

Printed in Poland
by Amazon Fulfillment
Poland Sp. z o.o., Wrocław